Sobornost

Sobornost
Eastern Unity of Mind and Heart
for Western Man

Catherine de Hueck Doherty

AVE MARIA PRESS
NOTRE DAME, INDIANA 46556

Library of Congress Catalog Card Number: 77-89078

International Standard Book Number: 0-87793-141-0 (Paper)
0-87793-142-9 (Cloth)

©1977 by Ave Maria Press, Notre Dame, Indiana 46556

Cover photo: Candida Photos, Inc.

Printed and bound in the United States of America.

Contents

Foreword

SOBORNOST

A strange word
In this strange land . . .
But yet one that is
The warp and woof
Of men's eternal dreams . . .

He came to make
This dream come true . . .
He died to make it
Palpable and touchable
By all . . .
Who but stretched
Their hands to hold it.

He promised that all
Who believe in him
Will be his body
And he their head,
Uniting God and man
In a unity-incredible,
That only could be the fruit
Of love.

Sobornost was born
Then—
When he arose from death
And sealed it
With his resurrection.

CHAPTER
1

A Strange, New Word

Slowly, yet seemingly inexorably, a new Russian word is making its way into the American and English language — *sobornost!* (Pronounced: so•bor'•nost)

What does it mean exactly, this strange word? So many wonder about it, as they did about "poustinia." Even my publishers weren't quite ready to accept *poustinia*, it seemed so alien. Even though it simply meant "a desert" in Russian, it frightened people. But I was very adamant and wouldn't let go of it — because it was part of my life, part of my soul, part of my Russian heritage. But the "Ave Maria Press" are lovely people and they accepted it and the book has become, at least among Christians, a more or less familiar word. But *sobornost?* That's a new one!

Literally, it means *unity,* and one of the publications from England dedicated to unity, or reunion, calls itself

Sobornost, and rightly so, because it seeks unity among all denominations.

But to Russians the word "sobornost" is a much deeper concept than just unity.

One can say a team is a symbol of unity in the West — a group who has decided to abide by certain rules of play or work and is very united on that particular part of their life. People can be united on political and economic unity or policy, but the word "sobornost" goes much deeper than all that. It means a unity that has passed through the gospel as a "gathering factor" — for in Russian, "sobornost" means "gathering."

Sobrania is related to "sobornost." The gathering usually is solemn and very important to those who "gather it" or get it together. So, in a manner of speaking, the Russian would say, "I participated in a *sobor*. . . . It was a wonderful *sobrania,* and it had a real *sobornost.*" Translated, this means that the person was at a vitally important meeting, and that the gathering (*sobrania*) was really handpicked, shall we say, because it had a real unity.

However true all this is, it is still very difficult to reach the immense depth of mind, soul and heart that is expressed by the word "sobornost." It is, to be absolutely truthful, when it exists, an *absolute unity* of, in this case, Christians. They think alike. They pray alike. They are alike. If one comes across such a group, it seems that they are looking at an icon of Christ. Each face is a composite of that icon, and the unity is soul-shaking, mind-blowing and earth-shaking. Certain sects have that sort of unity even though they might appear to be heretics to the majority of Christians. Alas, even amongst the sects the unity doesn't last very long. The Doukhobors, the Amish, and many, many others are often seduced into leaving their "sobornost," their unity.

Having said as much, I haven't said anything. Because I don't know how to explain, how to express, this total unity in which all those who are gathered by God into this *sobrania* (gathering) are of one mind on some immutable ideas which they accept, for example, "the Gospel without compromise." For us in Madonna House it is "the Little Mandate." On this we are a *sobrania* that automatically breeds sobornost.

How difficult are translations of words and ideas from one language to another. Still, I am forced to translate "sobornost." We must begin to know it, because, you see, it is part of the unity of Father, Son and Holy Spirit. It is from them, the perfection of sobornost, that we gather it. But the ingredients of sobornost are generations of breathing a certain air. Tolstoy and Dostoevsky tried to describe it, to portray it, but unless their writings are approached in grave humility, they become mere pieces of literary beauty; their very essence escapes the West. In the individualistic West, which grew more and more individualistic since the Renaissance (so-called), unity among people became rarer and rarer.

Few can agree on the gospel! Let us face the fact that unless we live the gospel—not only preach it, but *live it—there can be no unity among us,* no sobornost, no gathering of like minds. But in order to live the gospel, one has to move through the life of Jesus Christ. It means abandonment, being rejected, being crucified. There is no sobornost without crucifixion, because it is through pain that one acquires that deep knowledge that has nothing to do with books and education . . . that deep knowledge that is given by God and by God alone that builds the foundation of unity. People thus united are transparent, and it is in those depths that one finds, I repeat, the foundation of sobornost . . . of unity.

Sobornost is never superficial. It is never temporary. It is always there like cool water offered from the cup of one's heart to all of one's brethren.

Yes, there is much more to be said about sobornost!

CHAPTER 2

Experienced at Pentecost

Sobornost is really not a word but a concept, a dimension of God's grace, God's gift to man, for which they have hungered for a long, long time.

There was a moment in the history of mankind when a certain group of people experienced that gift, in a manner of speaking, and understood it with a heart flooded with such joy that other men who passed by thought they were drunk!

That day was Pentecost: the day when God's mercy and love came in the shape of tongues of fire and hovered over men's heads, filling them with unending joy, but also with the gifts of the Holy Spirit.

The Holy Spirit was indeed present to unite them, for Jesus Christ, only a little while before, had said in praying to his Father: ". . . that all of them may be one, Father, just as you are in me and I am in you." The Holy Spirit came on

Pentecost to begin that new dimension of unity which alone would enable men to follow the narrow path laid out by Jesus Christ and to understand what "sobornost"—what gathering—this really was.

The Holy Spirit was consolidating—if that word is applicable to the Most Holy Trinity—the teachings of the Lord. Here, on this immense holy day of the descent of the Holy Spirit upon the apostles was the opening of their hearts to the parables, the teachings: "Whatsoever you do to the least of my brethren you do to me." The beatitudes must have been illuminated by the tongues of fire: the slow flowering of the flower of love to loving God . . . to loving oneself . . . to loving one's neighbor . . . to loving one's enemies . . . to laying one's life down for everyone. Truly, the descent of the Holy Spirit on Pentecost brought light into the darkest corners of the apostles' hearts and from them kept on going from one heart to another heart as they preached the gospel and lived it.

Yes, there was a day in the history of mankind when "sobornost," the whole gathering, was truly the gathering of God and men.

But in order to reach Pentecost, the Lord Jesus Christ had to go through his incarnation, his death and his resurrection.

We come, as I always think, from the head of God and we move to the heart of God. That should be our life . . . a life that understands eternity because it looks at itself—physical, emotional and spiritual—in faith, and realizes (in faith, I repeat) that God has created us. It realizes, too, that we have sinned against him in one way or another. As Jung, the great psychiatrist, concluded after examining a large number of patients, Genesis is right: there was some kind of grievous fault that men committed against a greater power than themselves, a fault we have named "original sin."

The coming of Jesus Christ, his incarnation, death and resurrection, brought forth Baptism, and Baptism, by taking up our sins and instituting the sacraments, healed this original sin, and we come from it into a beautiful union with God again, as it used to be before the fall. A "sobornost" again between God and man, but this time on a great scale, for the Lord not only instituted the sacrament of Baptism, but he made us understand that we are part of his Mystical Body . . . and that he is our head . . . that our "sobornost" lies also in that realm, for if I am the hand of the Mystical Body, then I must be united to the body. *Am I?*

St. Paul brings to us again the new concept of "sobornost." He talks about people having all the gifts possible and imaginable: "If I speak in the tongues of men and angels. . . . If I have the gift of prophecy. . . . If I have faith. . . . If I give all I possess to the poor and surrender my body to the flames. . ." (1 Cor 13:1-4), but he ends very simply by telling us, if you have all these gifts and don't have love or charity, all these things are useless.

So we come back to Pentecost. As the Russians often call the Holy Spirit, "the Crimson Dove, the God of Love," he is the Advocate who advocates the totality of our love for God and for man. Thus, in truth, we can create a "sobornost."

CHAPTER 3

One in Mind and Heart

When we follow the counsels of the Holy Spirit, then we can create sobornost!

Today the Charismatic Movement is becoming awake to "sobornost," but they call it "community conscience." I think that God wants us to share in that "community conscience," and yet in my Russian mind he is shaping us into a sobornost: one group . . . one mind . . . united . . . solid . . . unafraid of risks and facing them with one mind. If there is a need to jump into an abyss, that "community conscience" that is beginning to be recognized slowly by some modern Christians begins truly to function. The faithful, the believers jump into the abyss as one.

You can see, for instance, what happened to Friendship House in Toronto and in Harlem. In Toronto we were subjected to an outside attack which was very obvious. It came from the public. In Harlem the attack came from the inside and was an insidious one, taking a long time to reveal itself. But in both cases it was the devil, and the only way to face the devil is *as one!*

Spiritually there should not be many Madonna Houses— *there should be only one!* Slowly we form ourselves into a sobornost, of which the "community conscience" is a part.

Sobornost stands guard over a little piece of paper which we call "the Little Mandate." And a "community conscience" abides by that piece of paper and will be quartered, crucified, die for it! Yes, all for that little three-by-five card we call our "Little Mandate."

For if your "community conscience" and mine leads us to sobornost, then truly no one can touch you. They can kill you but they can't kill the spirit that is yours. For each one of us who is willing to die, 10 will arise to continue holding high the torch of it, like the young person who holds the torch of the Olympic games, passing it from generation to generation.

Still, we have to discuss sobornost a little more deeply, for its incarnation in daily life becomes the source of "community conscience."

The most perfect sobornost exists, of course, in the Most Holy Trinity, and when God created man and woman, before the fall, it existed between man, woman and God. As long as Adam and Eve did the will of God they were in unity with him. God and men were united in tremendous bonds of love.

As I have already said, there was a break in that unity. The break occurred between man and God, for man broke that unity. Yet even though he had destroyed it, he hungered for it all through the ages. And, as we have seen, through the incarnation, suffering and resurrection of Christ came the immense gift of reunion and friendship with God again. The sobornost was again established through Baptism and enlarged by the Eucharist. Both sacraments seal God's unity with man and man's unity with God.

Here I am trying to explain the unexplainable, because factually sobornost is a mystery, deeply hidden in the heart of God and given as a gift to men. Yes, it is a mystery, and the only way to pierce God's mysteries is by listening to his voice, doing his will and praying.

Listening and praying must obviously be reflected in the life of the Christian, for the law of Christ must be incarnated in man. "To serve and to pray" still remains the foundation of all sobornost.

This becomes very obvious when we turn to the West and look at the 11th century, when the Benedictines rose to their height in power and possessions. At that time, the Cistercians in France renewed the Church by a simple way of life based on what to the Russian would be a "community conscience" leading to sobornost. They were all of one mind in deciding that the best way to renew the Church was to work and pray. Simple, humble work is what they embraced and by doing so they renewed the fire of Jesus Christ on earth. This simplicity in which the fire was enclosed affected the whole Middle Ages for some 300 years or more.

Here I am wrestling with words, trying to make a mystery understandable to the East as well as to the West, because it seems that God wants me to do that. But frankly I would like to throw all the fancy words out of my vocabulary and approach sobornost on my knees, but with a tremendous joy because the tongues of fire have hovered over me, too. The

Baptism by water and by the Spirit is clearly stated in the gospel, and so I, too, have had my Pentecost. I, too, am heir to the gifts of the Holy Spirit. I, too, have to try to explain sobornost without explaining it because it is something that one's heart catches from another heart—a sort of fire—for God has sent his fire, the Holy Spirit, as an Advocate, but also to clean all the dross from human hearts, to make them free so that in total faith, trust and love, they might turn to one another. And, one could say, by not holding hands, but by holding one another's hearts, they blend with the heart of Christ.

Sobornost is God's way for us to deal with the emergencies that confront us. Sobornost is there to face the enemy who is constantly attacking all the works of God in the hearts of men as well as in society.

Sobornost is the restoration, the healing of wounds inflicted on his body.

Yes, sobornost is the gathering of the faithful (*sobrania*) in time of emergencies. At other times the "community conscience" of a family, of an institution, of a religious order, of a people, should function, for it takes its roots in the sobornost—the unity of God and man.

CHAPTER 4

United Through Fire

The American and Canadian Indians seem to have understood sobornost much better than Christians. I picked up, the other day, a little pamphlet entitled *Four Remarkable Indian Prophecies* and this is what I read. "We also have a religion which was given by our forefathers and has been handed on to us, their children. It teaches us to be thankful, *to be united,* and to love one another. We never argue about religion" (from a speech of Red Jacket, a famous Seneca orator).

There is more. "It is my personal belief, after 35 years' experience of it, that there is no such thing as 'Christian civilization!' I believe that Christianity and modern civilization are opposed irreconcilably and that the spirit of Christianity and our ancient religion is essentially the same" (Charles Eastman, Sioux Indian doctor).

"They (our group of missionaries) told us that only their denomination was right and all the others were wrong. We asked ourselves, how can this be? All these people say that they believe in the Great Maker and in the same Prophet (Jesus) but they quarrel with one another. Surely that is not godliness" (from a speech of Nipo Strongheart, orator of the Yakima).

Perhaps I should say at this point that my spiritual director for several years has urged me to write the best I could about this tremendous mystery of sobornost, and I have always felt totally inadequate to do so.

But he insisted, and I truly believe in obeying one's spiritual director, so I kept on praying and eventually I came to understand that whatever I write about sobornost will be inspired by God, in a manner of speaking, because I realize the mystery of it, because I approach this task with deep prayer and consider the will of my spiritual director to be the will of God.

Slowly, not without pain, this outline is seeing the light of day.

Of course, I seek to gather the wisdom of the Christian East and the Christian West, but once in a while I come across what they call "ancient religions"—in this case that of the North American Indians—and I stand in awe before the ways of God who is the Lord of History, and who slowly leads people to himself through various and marvelous ways, some of them already redolent with Christian principles.

The Russians have an extraordinary love of and affinity for the Holy Spirit. A quick perusal of Eastern liturgies and Russian prayers will convince anyone, for they are filled with repetitive prayers and petitions and love of the Holy Spirit.

True, the Russians think of him always in context with the Most Holy Trinity, but also they have realized very clearly his role in the life of a Christian.

That is why they plunge deeply into his fire, realizing that they have to catch sparks of it if they are going to incarnate the promises of their Baptism.

They know, too, that it will be the Holy Spirit who will help them to make themselves an icon of Christ since they constantly partake of his body and blood. He will keep them on the "straight and narrow path" of which the Lord speaks. And, above all, he will forge the bond of unity amongst the faithful, bonds of fire and strength, bonds of reality that faces its Baptism squarely!

For Baptism, we know, is the dying with Christ and the resurrecting with Christ—but this dying and this resurrecting are constant. That is the reality of sobornost, too, as well as the reality of Christianity. To follow Christ is a tremendous risk. To follow Christ is to tear out by the roots the shrubs of one's own will and put them into a fire that really consumes and plants the seeds of God's will, which, as they grow, will mold our lives.

So let's face it. Let us face it as a family, as an organization, as a community (religious or lay), as citizens of various countries. As peoples, let us face it, for we will have to enter the mystery of the Holy Spirit who is God's love burning over us and in us like tongues of fire. It is through this fire, and through this fire alone, that we can become one in mind, heart and even emotions.

CHAPTER 5

An Exchange of Hearts

After looking at what I have written, suddenly I wish I could communicate what my heart feels about sobornost. To me it always comes back, not as a theological verity—which it is—nor as a concept or idea over which we can cerebrate, but as a mystery.

Yes, sobornost is a mystery, obviously to be understood by the heart. Factually, it is *obvious* that it is a mystery, because it is the mystery of union between not only men and men, peoples and peoples, but between God and people.

Sobornost is a mystery, but it is a mystery of love. One doesn't penetrate love with one's mind, with one's head, because the head is absolutely useless for love. Nor is love part of what you might call emotions. Yes, it has an emotional overtone and there are emotional situations, especially when we talk about sexual love. But we are not talking about sexual love. We are talking about something so strange, so mysterious, so incredible that one's head begins to spin when one thinks about it, meditates on it and especially contemplates it.

It is like looking into a body of water and suddenly seeing the waters open up in some kind of infinite silvery depths, at the bottom of which is the face of Christ. It might be an icon, but to you it is Christ's face, and the strangest thing happens, an absolutely incredible thing happens when you look down. *His face reflects the face of the Father.* This happens, of course, because he said, "Whoever has seen me has seen the Father" (Jn 14:9). But now *his face reflects also your face and my face.*

That is truly a mystery, and it is by looking, and I repeat, contemplating this strange phenomenon that one begins to understand sobornost—this oneness that I am trying to talk about. This oneness is my seeing the face of Christ and he reflecting my face. That is the way it comes to me.

It comes to me in another way, also. It comes to me in the bending—yes, you know, in the bending—the way the Russians bend and kneel down to kiss the floor or lie flat on it.

You must understand what that means, for man doesn't stand as he is in the fullness of his height before God. He bends. He adores, and it is expressed by his movements.

Yes, I think of sobornost as "bending." Bending to kiss the face of Christ which reflects my face, but at the same time reflects the face of God the Father and his face.

What does it mean, this "bending"? It means surrender. It means that I acknowledge who I am and who God is. For once the proud spirit of the 20th century, of our technological age, suddenly realizes that all its arrogance is a lot of foolishness, to put it mildly. And it doesn't work!

Yet man begins to bend lower and lower and lower until he knows with every part of his body—his muscles, his heart, his emotions, his conscience—that he is one with God if he does the will of God.

Yes, now he understands, and his bending turns to prostration, for again the blinding knowledge of who God is and who he is has become a reality in him and now the roles have been defined.

God is God and I am a man or woman, a person. He is the Creator and I am his creature. *It is good to know that!* It is the beginning of sobornost. Believe it or not, it is the beginning of sobornost because now I can rise from this posture of being down . . . down . . . down . . . of being flat on my face. I can rise, for now I have become a child, because I have understood who God is and who I am. Such a joy pervades me that I feel like a child, and so I begin to dance and sing and play games with God as a child would. It is thus that sobornost grows in me. Grows and grows and grows. Why? Because I have found God in me, in the right proportion. Yes, now I can rise. Now I can dance and play with God. Now I can be a child.

Don't you see why sobornost grows and grows? Because children trust. Children are of one mind with parents and elders—little children—Christ's children. Don't you see? They really proceed to do the will of the Father. And sobornost grows and grows and grows.

As I said before, now their hearts are open. Why? Because the light of love has penetrated them. Now I can take your heart and you can take my heart and we can exchange hearts. Like some saints exchanged their hearts with God's heart, we can do likewise. We can exchange hearts, and when we exchange hearts, then we are one.

But how are you going to put that? How are you going to make people understand that sort of thing? Everybody in this pragmatic, cerebral society always wants to put himself first, and this cannot be done. God doesn't want me to do it. God wants me to be *third,* never first. God comes first, my neighbor second, and I am third!

Well, I was musing about sobornost and wondering if a theological approach, a conceptual approach, a philosophical approach would do. And my heart answered me that it wouldn't, for this is how I felt about sobornost. This is how the song of sobornost sings in me.

But the question is, how am I going to tell it to the Madonna House staff, to its visitors, to the world, if each seems to be pursued by his own desires. Terrorists and non-terrorists, governments and people in general, shopkeepers and customers, parents and children, religious communities of men and women, lay apostolates and so on down the line are all involved in doing "their thing"! So my song of sobornost doesn't sing to them. They don't seem to be listening to God but to themselves, and there is a sort of cacophony in their hearts or ears. It shouldn't be that way, but it is.

Yes, that's how I see the real foundation of sobornost: my reflection in God's face; my surrender (bending) to him and his will, leading to the exchange of hearts with him and with my brothers and sisters in him; arising from the "bending" with the song of sobornost in my heart and at last *becoming a child,* "I assure you that unless you change and become like children, you will never enter the kingdom of heaven" (Mt 18:3).

CHAPTER 6

The "Fiat" of a Jewish Maid

Sobornost is mind-blowing. It shatters all human preconceived ideas. It tears apart all conceptual postulates. It plays havoc with what would be considered mental law and order. It enters the intellect to show it that it has wings that must be folded, and it comes to fold them by blowing as once upon a time God came in a gentle breeze.

Yes, all this mind-blowing . . . all this mind-folding . . . comes from God. Why? Because God hungers for man's love just as man hungers for God's love. St. Augustine said, "Our hearts are restless until they rest in thee." The incredible thing, the mind-blowing thing is that God reciprocates.

This hunger for God takes palpable shape and physical shape in prayer, for prayer is both palpable and physical, even though its roots are deep in the mysterious hearts of men. Sobornost expresses itself in the West through the Prayer of the Presence of God, which is a standing still before God, realizing his presence inside and outside oneself. It is a powerful prayer. It is a prayer that doesn't need a special place in which to be prayed. The world is its chapel. It can be prayed in a streetcar, while talking, while walking, while lecturing. Because it is the supreme act of man loving God and being aware of him, it is a prayer without words.

Sobornost expresses itself in the East through the Jesus Prayer, which begins with a constant repetition of the Name of Jesus and with the addition at first of "Lord, have mercy on me a sinner." It is recited like a mantra, a repetitious prayer that has rhythm . . . the rhythm that breath has. Breathe in, breathe out, and recite the prayer rhythmically as you do. But soon it ceases to be something that you can do, and it becomes something that you live. One is lost in the awesome, holy Presence of God—for the Jesus Prayer brings God as vividly before the soul as the Prayer of the Presence of God. Now it becomes part and parcel of one's life, so much so that even sleep does not interrupt it for "I sleep and my heart watcheth."

It is prayed almost as if God prayed in you. There is no explanation for it. It just is. With every sentence which ceases to be a sentence but is breath and life, one comes closer and closer and closer to God until God and you, God and I, are united in a sobornost that nothing can break.

In a way both for the West and the East, the Prayer of the Presence of God and the Jesus Prayer are keys to silence. In this silence we find out who we truly are.

Sobornost uses the scriptures, of course, especially the Gospels. Sobornost listens to Jesus Christ constantly. We mean that people who desire sobornost are scripture-readers and gospel-doers, who listen constantly to the Holy Spirit.

But the silence I speak of this time, the result of the Prayer of the Presence of God or of the Jesus Prayer, this silence is the ultimate silence, the one that listens to Yahweh as well as to Jesus Christ and the Holy Spirit. To be absolutely direct, it is the silence that allows men to enter the Trinity, for whenever we listen to one Person we listen to the others. But it takes the grace of God, a special gift of the Holy Spirit, to be able to hear the voice of the Trinity, the Trinity, which is the perfect sobornost, and which speaks with perfect unity.

Sobornost is strengthened by the ways we have just described of approaching God. Yes, it is strengthened because now we can touch God. Jesus Christ said to Mary Magdalene when she first met him on the morning of his resurrection, "Do not touch me, for I have not yet returned to the Father" (Jn 20:17).

But now with the Prayer of the Presence of God and the Jesus Prayer soaring through our hearts like a thousand fingers, like a million eyes, we can touch Christ with those fingers, we can embrace him with those eyes, and "He who sees me sees the Father." So, in a strange and mysterious way, again we touch the Trinity.

Yes, sobornost is composed of faith and prayer, love and hope. But we are weak. We are frightened. Somehow we know that if we embark on the road of sobornost we are embarking on the road of risk and pain and surrender.

We look around to find a model. Our heart shouts. Our mind weeps: "Where is that model?" If only we could see someone practice it—this strange word that comes to us from a strange country—Russia—sobornost! We of the North American continent are not familiar with all those things and so often we allow sobornost to pass through our fingers while they are lifted in prayer. Fingers can be sieves, too.

Ah, we haven't looked far enough, deep enough or high enough. We haven't looked at a Jewish maid. A woman to whom an angel came and announced the incredible tidings, "Hail Mary, full of grace! The Lord is with thee." And when she asked him what he meant, this strange angel, he said she would be overshadowed by the Holy Spirit: "The Holy Spirit will come upon you, and the power of the Most High will overshadow you. So the Holy One to be born will be called the Son of God" (Lk 1:35). He implied that what she was going to conceive came from God.

Ha, here comes the crunch. Here comes the totality of faith. Listen: "Behold the handmaid of the Lord. Be it done to me according to thy word"!

Here is the perfection of sobornost. We said before that the perfection of sobornost was in the Most Holy Trinity. The three persons think as one and act as one. But now, a creature like yourself, like myself, a 14-year-old girl speaks a single little word, a single word that has reechoed throughout the whole earth and will reecho to the end of time. It is that word that brought those who are lovers of God to cry out with her, *"Fiat—be it done to me according to thy word."*

Let us follow her a little further because she is like me, like you; she is like all creatures. She isn't like God. She is created. She is the model we have been looking for, the model we can hang on to, follow and achieve the same totality of unity of our will with God's will.

So she brought forth a child. She faced the situation with St. Joseph and she remained silent. The Lord spoke to St. Joseph. She didn't. She hoped the Lord would speak to him and her hope became incarnated through the dream of St. Joseph. She must have loved St. Joseph, but she understood she had to keep her virginity. That was a love that wove in her heart sobornost like one weaves a cloth. Perhaps that is what went into that seamless robe that even the Romans wouldn't cut, but threw dice for.

And so the child was born and for an unknown number of years, say 30, according to the Gospel, she must have wondered who that Child of hers was.

But sobornost expressed itself in little things done very well by the Son of God, working very humbly as a carpenter, and by his mother. Then one day he disappeared, in a manner of speaking. Did he say good-bye to her or didn't he—probably he did—but that's not important. The important thing is the center, the essence, of that strange woman who gave birth to the Son of God, who lived with him for 30 years in the totality of surrender to the will of the Father, and when he left, she followed him from far away, understanding his seeming rejection of her at one point when he said he had no mother and no father. Here too she "bended" as the Russians bend. It might not have been physical but it was inward. Her whole person "bended." Her soul "bended" and she probably repeated once more, "Be it done to me according to Thy word." Once more the "fiat" rang across the world. This time in total silence, perhaps. But one can say "fiat" in silence, too.

And then he preached. She followed him from afar. She met him one day as he was wending his way to Golgotha, so the legends say, but these legends are tradition, deeply imbedded in the soul of man. For a moment she held him, clumsily, him and the cross. And then he was gone. She stood under the cross. For those who have ears to hear, the "fiat" she must have repeated and repeated constantly was not only a song of mourning but a song of gladness because at that moment she must have understood that by becoming the mother of God she became the mother of men.

But perhaps this was just a nebulous thought when suddenly his voice sounded above her and he confirmed it, saying to John the Beloved who was also standing under the cross, "Behold your mother." And to her he said, "Behold your son." And the nebulous thought that must have come to her was clarified. She knew with her whole being that she was the mother of all men as well as the mother of God. She tasted martyrdom. That is why tradition calls her the Queen of Martyrs!

She sat down. On what? A stone? A piece of wood? We can't tell. They put her dead Son into her arms, and she became the Pieta. Her human heart might have been broken, but the face of the Pieta is serene because now she knew—she knew who she was and why the Son of God had been born to her. She knew that she was going to be the ultimate example of sobornost. She was going to be sobornost itself, for while Adam and Eve walked with God in the cool of the evening, and talked to him in the garden, she was the new Eve. She held God in her arms, and her will and his will were one.

If we listen carefully we will know that the Prayer of the Presence of God and the Jesus Prayer blend into one when they touch Mary. They become a song in which "fiat" and "alleluia" blend constantly.

CHAPTER 7

Trinity: Fire, Flame, Motion

It seems that in this book on sobornost there are moments when I write with my mind, with my intellect, and moments when I don't. The moments when I don't are really pleasant, for I seem to enter into a void which is extremely relaxing but also extremely awesome, because the Holy Spirit seems to be deeply present within my heart. At those moments I think he is the one writing!

But, of course, this must be an illusion. Illusion or not, it makes me feel as if I were on my knees, with the Lord himself teaching me. He, of course, is the best source of all history, all theology, all philosophy.

But, back to sobornost. Now I want to talk about the Most Holy Trinity.

Dearly beloved friends of God, if there is a mystery about sobornost, there is an infinitely greater mystery in the Trinity, which no one can explain. I certainly can't, but, strangely enough, there is in the Trinity this quiet void which urges me on. Yes, in this quiet void everything seems to be so urgent, for a void can be urgent; it can tell you in a thousand voices, "Go ahead! Why shouldn't you go ahead? You can talk about the Trinity because you love it. That is the only reason." Those who walk around in an enchanted circle of theology, history, philosophy, and of this and of that, can't penetrate it at all if they confine themselves to their own intellects.

But it's so nice . . . so nice to think about the Trinity in relation to sobornost. It is as if the house in Nazareth opened up and there were Mary and Joseph and Jesus, and the supper was laid out on the table and another sobornost met our eyes, for these three were also of the same mind and heart.

Yes, suddenly our eyes are opened and we see the invisible Trinity which Rublev painted as three angels having supper. It is a strange icon. Perhaps it is the most beautiful expression of the "Holy" ever made. Rublev was a Russian, but his Trinity has captured the hearts of millions of people . . . people who understood art, and people who understood something more than art and who know that icon painters depart at times into a deep void in which their icons are painted by another hand and, in a manner of speaking, they just copy what is in front of the eyes of their heart. Yes, that's the way it happens sometimes.

So, what about the Trinity? Well, first and foremost, the Trinity appears to me like fire and flame and eternal motion. The motion translates itself in my heart as creation, and creation is an eternal movement. People who create, move.

The Trinity is creative. Fire, flame and a movement

which is at the same time inward and outward! Then, quite suddenly, or not so suddenly, the movement, the fire, the flame, part like a curtain on a stage and somehow or other I enter a fantastic realm of faith, faith that I didn't even know existed. Now I see—without seeing. Now I hear—without hearing. I believe with a flaming belief, a belief that seems to rise from my heart to the heart of God!

CREDO! . . . Credo that there are three Persons in the Trinity. Yes, the flaming, moving, fiery curtain parts, yet I don't see three persons. I don't see a man with a beard, a youth and a Spirit hovering over them like a dove. None of these things I see but in faith I know that as this fiery curtain for a second parts, I behold Unity!

I behold what the Creed says, "three in one." Incredible, isn't it? Yes, "Three in one, and one in three." Now I know the perfection of unity. Now I know what sobornost is: the song of God! All beauty is the echo of God's voice, for all music sung by God is based on the theme of unity between Father, Son and Holy Spirit. In the midst of this unity abides Mary. She isn't of the Trinity, of course, but she is surrounded by it in a most intimate way, for her "fiat" still resounds both in heaven and on earth, an example to all the faithful.

Then I see the Trinity encompass men. It is very difficult, for when you are in the void, things are a little different, and so are words. Once again I mean by the word "encompass" that the Trinity is one, and the song of the Trinity is based on this unity—that is why music (good music) is a unifying aspect of life among people. On earth everybody understands music. But do you know something? The devil can hear, too, and he tries to bring his cacophony into this music of unity. He really does!

Anyhow, from the Trinity comes the music of unity. From the Trinity comes peace, for Jesus said, "Peace I leave with you; my peace I give you. I do not give it to you as the world gives. Do not let your hearts be troubled and do not be afraid" (Jn 14:27). You have to take that into consideration.

At first this peace seems to us unpeace, for it spells total surrender of our will to God's will, a readiness to become at any time a martyr, a holocaust for the people of God. It also spells acceptance of pain as if it were in truth the kiss of Christ, as a spiritual writer called it. Yes, we have to consider Christ's peace. If we accept it in its reality, with all its risks, in all its totality, then we shall know freedom and joy and begin to soar not only to the top of the Holy Mountain but beyond that into the heart of the Trinity.

So when Christ said, "My peace I give you," which actually is the peace of the Father also, and of the Holy Spirit, he at the same time gave us the Holy Spirit because the Most Holy Trinity foresaw that we would be afraid of that peace of the Trinity.

The Triune God bade us to love. To behold what the Trinity bade us to do is to understand dimiy what love is . . . thin, like a sliver, yet for all that thinness it always is a movement, a fire, a flame. Yes, that is our love. That is its essence. It embraces friend and enemy. It lays its life down while it sings its alleluias of forgiveness to those who want to take that life. It cherishes not what is its own, but gives it away with a lavish hand. It is enamored of poverty, but above all it is enamored of the God of the poor. Yes, from it springs everything that exists, for it is the love of the Most Holy Trinity that brought forth everything that exists, including our hearts that reflect, or should, theirs.

One more thing has to be understood, that God is father and mother to everything that exists, from the incredible riches of heaven, its stars, galaxies, and constellations, to our little planet earth.

Yes, the Trinity is the seed of love, and from it springs its foundations: peace, love, music, for all are foundations for sobornost, for the unity of man with the Trinity. For didn't Yahweh say, "Can a mother forget her infant, be without tenderness for the child of her womb? Even if she forget, I will never forget you" (Is 49:15).

CHAPTER 8

A New Creation

If anyone is in Christ he is a new creation. The old order has passed away; now all is new! All this has been done by God who reconciled us to himself through Christ and has given us the ministry of reconciliation.

I mean that God in Christ was reconciling the world to himself, not counting men's transgressions against him and he has entrusted the message of reconciliation to us. That makes us ambassadors for Christ. God, as it were, *appealing through us. We implore you in Christ's name* to be reconciled to God. . . (2 Cor 5:17-20).

Yes, St. Paul put it in a nutshell! If we are in Christ, we are a new creation. That is, of course, also the heart of sobornost. Those who truly understand sobornost, or try to, *know* that to be part of sobornost one must be a new creation!

Sobornost, which we have discussed in its many aspects, is the expression of a human heart and it is God who orchestrates the human heart, and it is he who has done what St. Paul says; all of it he has done because he has reconciled us to himself through Christ!

Let us meditate, contemplate, enter into the depth of this tremendous thought, of this tremendous verity, of this new dimension that is ours because of the goodness of God.

It is God who has reconciled us and it is through Jesus Christ that he has done so. Jesus, obedient unto death, the death of the cross, took our sins upon himself, for only thus could we be reconciled to God.

And now, because Christ has done so, we also have the gift of reconciliation, that is to say, to reconcile ourselves with ourselves, to reconcile ourselves with our brethren. We have to become ambassadors of God, of forgiveness and reconciliation. The same way as God dealt with us through Jesus Christ we must now deal with others and this, of course, *is* sobornost. For to help men to reconcile themselves with one another, that is the work of God in us. Without him we could not do it, but he *challenges* us to do it. It's not something we can take up and let go, oh no! It is part and parcel of our Baptism, our new nature, since we are now a new creation, as St. Paul so succinctly put it.

Yes, that's the way it should be. But is it? Do we understand that we are a new creation? Are we ready for the risk of reconciling ourselves with ourselves, brother to brother, people to people? That's a tough job. I spoke of risk, and sobornost demands risk because it leads us to unplumbed depths and unknown heights!

In the process of doing what St. Paul says we should do, we are rebuked, maligned, misunderstood, rejected—it is as if the devil bent down into the sea of human emotions and by the handful started throwing them at us! All hell breaks loose in our souls and even in our minds. The words of the scriptures seem to be erased. Even the luminous words of Christ as he goes about giving his parables which are the light to our feet and to our neighbors' feet, that light gets dimmed and we want to hide—hide either behind a line of sophistication or indifference, or beneath new easier religions or beneath none. Anything is grist to our mill when it comes to confrontation.

Yes, perhaps the word isn't "confronting" but "incarnating" the gospel. From this we shy away. Instead of praying for courage or crying out loudly, "Lord, out of the depths I cry to thee; hear the voice of my supplication. Give me courage! I believe. Help my unbelief!"—we don't utter a word. We turn our back to the risk and the joy of this ministry and we hide! But it doesn't really matter where we hide or how. For God always opens new avenues. Even in our "hiding" God makes new paths. There is the poustinia. It is such a nice place in which to hide. It is, these days, "respectable." In fact, there is an aura of holiness around and about it. People who haven't been in the poustinia look at one who has and say, "Oh, you have been in the poustinia? You don't mean to say that you are going there every week!"

One can easily answer in the affirmative because so many do go weekly across the world these days. It is a good place to hide. You can read a little bit of the scriptures and go to sleep, relax, take a little walk, and the fast even helps. You lose a little weight maybe, or if you don't, we feel virtuous, and the confrontation that looks at us from each corner of the poustinia—for we know that it does—can be shut off by sleeping, by fasting, and by daydreaming which sometimes is mistaken for prayer.

Strangely enough, whether hiding place or open place, the poustinia is reached by a sort of pilgrimage. It is the eager pilgrimage of youth . . . and of middle age and old age, for the Lord doesn't care about physical age. He cares about childlikeness. And so those who have a childlike heart suddenly, be they young, middle-aged, or old, inwardly, inside themselves, seem to hear a voice saying, "Arise and come." And so they do. Yes, they do arise and they go on an inner pilgrimage that eventually will lead them to a poustinia. One doesn't take too much luggage, but what one takes is soon taken away from us.

Yes, I have written a poem about that.

JOURNEY INWARD

My soul hungered
For God
Before it was clothed
With flesh.

But when it became
Imprisoned
In the flesh that is
I
It fell asleep.

And those who sleep
Know hunger not.

Somewhere along
The road of life
By the grace of
God,
My soul woke up

And its hunger
Now,
Became a fire.

A fire that consumed
Me.
Ate me up
With its intense
Devouring heat.

I could not rest
Anywhere
Except in motion,

In a motion that
Led me to God.

That is how I
Began
The journey inward.

That long, endless
Journey
That every soul
Must undertake

If she is to meet
Her God.

It is a strange
Journey,
Across arid plains,
And verdant valleys,
Dried parchment-like
Deserts.

A journey of
Twisting, narrow
Roads,
Now leading
Upwards,
Now downwards.

A journey of many
Crossroads
And endless
Sharp turns

That confuse
And clamor
For a rest.

But the hunger
For God
Knows no rest.
So I go on,
And on, and on.

Yes, it is a strange
Journey,
That slowly
Makes me shed
All the baggage
I took for it

The baggage I took
For it,
Before I knew
That it was
Too heavy a load
For this kind of
Journey.

I don't know where
I left it.
Somewhere
Back there
By some crossroad.

Now I am baggage-less
But somehow
Still too heavily
Burdened,

My hunger drives me
On.

But now for speedy
Traveling it
Demands,

I must start
Shedding my
Clothing.

There, on this stone
I must lay
The cloak
Of selfishness
That kept me warm.

It is cold
Without it,
But I can walk
Faster,
As my hunger
Urges me
To.

Here, on this branch
I must hang
My dress of
Self-love
And compromise
With the world.

I shiver now,
In earnest
But my feet
Seem to have
Wings.

Yet this sheltered
Rock
Begs for my
Underwear.

Slowly, reluctantly
I shed one by one
My undergarments—
Here goes self-
Indulgence.

Tidily, next to it,
I lay greed for
Possessions, and
Love of ease and

Next, not so
Tidily go
Helter-skelter
All the things
In me that are
Not God's.

Lord, behold
I stand naked
Before Thee,
With wings on
My feet.

With wings on
My feet.
Now my journey
Inward
Will be swift.

But it is
Not.
For I still
Stumble
And fall, and
Walk haltingly
Inches, instead of
Miles.

While the hunger for
God
Flays me and
Urges me to make
Haste.

Oh, I had forgotten
The shoes —
The heavy, comfortable
Shoes
That have shielded
My feet.

Shielded my feet
From the cutting
Stones.
From the sharp
Pebbles.

I must unlace
My shoes.
My comfortable
Stout shoes.

The last covering
Of my naked body.
The last stronghold
Of my non-surrender
To God.

I hesitate.
The narrow path
Upwards
Is so hard.

It has so many
So many sharp
Stones.

So many knife-edged
Pebbles.

But the hunger
For God
Flames in me
A furnace of fire
Unquenchable.

The fire of love
Of passionate
Utter love
Of God.

I must go on
On that journey
Inward
That alone
Will bring me
Face to Face

With him
For whom I hunger
Constantly
Without ceasing.

Quickly I bend
With hasty clumsy
Fingers
I unlace one
Shoe
Then the other.

My eagerness
Is becoming part
Of my hunger

Recklessly
I throw
One shoe — this way
The other — that.

Not caring
Whither which falls
And now
I am free.

I am free
And naked
And my feet
Have huge wings

Huge wings
That carry me
Across the sharp
Stones

And the knife-edged
Pebbles
Without harm

Now brambles and
Thorns that edge
The path
Open up
And point
The other way.

I am a naked
Soul
Free and untrammeled
Driven by the
Hunger of my love
For God.

Driven by my love for
God . . . on and on . . .
On this journey
Inward.

I did not know
It was going to
Be so easy
Now that I
Shed all my
Garments

But now I *know*
For my hunger is
Being assuaged
Satiated — filled
Even as I fly
On my winged feet.

Along the steep
Path upward.
It is being filled
That hunger of mine
So much, so well.

That I can feed
Others
With the surplus
Of the food given to me
So abundantly.

Yes, my soul hungered
For God,
Before it was even
Clothed with flesh

God meets
The soul
That starts
On its journey inward
Half way.

Provided the soul
Driven by its
Hunger of love
For him
Strips itself
Naked.

That is the secret
Of his love
And of his kingdom
That begins
Even on this earth.

But the price
I repeat
Is *Nakedness*
Complete.
Even Unto
Discarding
Shoes . . .

This pilgrimage which came to me in the form of a poem is really the foundation of sobornost, which lets go of everything, all preconceived notions, all fears, all hesitation, and will eventually lead to poustinia and from thence . . . well, we shall see!

CHAPTER 9

An Inner Pilgrimage

I must confess that the writing of *Sobornost* is harder than the writing of *Poustinia,* perhaps because it goes deeper. Of course poustinia has endless depths and endless heights, but you reach them slowly, whereas with sobornost it is rather suddenly that you come upon them—the truths that are the foundations of sobornost—and it blows your mind. It really blows your mind, and yet it doesn't, because it's perfectly natural . . . in a supernatural way.

Of course here the difficulty lies: once you enter into poustinia, sobornost, pilgrimages, you are moving in the sphere of the supernatural, and the supernatural becomes natural, if you follow what I mean, and you have almost forgotten, or so it seems, that there was nature. Of course the supernatural builds on nature, but somehow or other, there is a mystery in that you enter the supernatural, and at that moment you suddenly forget the natural. That doesn't mean you are outside nature. It simply means, so I think, that the Lord is opening to you a new dimension, a new dimension of existence that you did not suspect.

In the last chapter, I explained the pilgrimage that leads to the poustinia. It's a strange pilgrimage which I tried to describe in a poem I composed when I faced my own pilgrimage in depth someplace in Rhode Island.

I was lecturing to the Madames of the Sacred Heart on Smith Street, Providence, and I couldn't sleep. So I went to the chapel, and that's where I got the idea of pilgrimage. I came back to my room and wrote the poem and sent it to my spiritual director. That's how it came to be. But it stayed in my heart, this poem. As time went by I reread the poem and realized that it was really the story of my life and the foundation of sobornost. It tells in poetic form of dropping everything that isn't God's in me and in you, and in all of us. We have so much baggage or luggage, or whatever you want to call it. We have a funny idea of pilgrimage. True, the hippies took very little with them on their peregrinations. But then they had homes, they had families, they had possessions elsewhere, although they tried to be pilgrims. The pilgrimage is not giving away only possessions and homes and all that sort of stuff like real pilgrims do. It's going deeper. It's as if you have an idea about pilgrimage, and it's a beautiful idea. Like the youth of the 60's, you take a knapsack and you proceed to do the best you can with jeans, bare feet or not, and you crisscross distances and go even to India, to all over the world in search of a dream—in search of truth, whatever it may be.

But a real pilgrimage is entered in a different way. Anyone who wants to be a pilgrim must first and foremost, if he is young and his parents are alive, ask the blessing of his father and mother, because without their blessing it doesn't work. Then he or she goes to the parish priest and gets his blessing. Now with a heart full of blessings he leaves, not taking anything. He's not going on a pilgrimage to a shrine or a monastery! He's going on an *inner* pilgrimage, slowly to become naked even as Christ became naked on the cross.

You have nothing left to cover yourself with, not even shoes, and it is then that you begin to see and understand. It is then that you are ready to preach the gospel . . . then the stones stop being sharp, the thorns turn another way, as I said in my poem, and you can share what is given you so abundantly with others. But what is given you so abundantly? A very simple thing. You have been cleansed. The healing, loving hand of Jesus Christ touched all of you. Did you have a fever? It cured you. Were you leprous? You became clean. Were you dead? You rose from the dead. A fantastic, incredible mystery took place. You are not the person that you were! No! You are not the person that you were.

Now you have a clean heart, the heart of a child, and you lift it up to God and like our Lady you say, "Let it be done to me according to thy word." You surrender like our Lord did. For a moment perhaps you, like he, asked, "Let this chalice pass by me," but immediately you continued as he did, "not my will be done, but yours." And so you are not the same person that you were. You are now a person whose *will* is blended with God's will. In fact, his will and your will are one and you desire only what he desires. You do not try to bring your will and his will into a strange clash. Not any more. That's all gone. You are united to him, and then sobornost begins to grow in your heart, and you are able to pass it on to others.

It's not as simple as all that, however, though it's simple enough. You see, the journey inward, the pilgrimage, the inner pilgrimage, leads to poustinia. Not a poustinia built by human hands like an *isba,* or a cabin, or a room in some place. No, again, it's an *inner* poustinia. It is a poustinia that has been made through your pilgrimage; this pilgrimage has made your heart empty, simple—a place where you can rest in peace, for nothing distracts you—no falderals . . . nothing. Your heart is like the real poustinia, a place to sleep on the floor, a kitchen table on which to read the scriptures and absorb them like food is absorbed.

But really it isn't at all a building of any kind. No. It's just within your heart that you have made the poustinia. It's within your heart that simplicity shines like a light. It is within your heart that the latch is open always to anyone who wants to come in, and especially to God who loves to come and rest in a poustinia like that. Here in this poustinia, notwithstanding the fact that friends and strangers, and even God, may visit it, you have to undergo the flowering of your Baptism, whether you have been baptized as a child or as an adult.

Slowly, and yet quite clearly, the Spirit will teach you, for Christ baptized in water and in the Spirit, and the Spirit will teach you. He will teach you the infinite riches of the Church of the Lord, the Church that was born out of his side, the Church of which he became the head, the Church which is his Mystical Body, the Church which is the salvation of the nations. In this poustinia you will know what the Church is and you will know what God asks of you, for himself, for the people of God that form the Church, for the world. He asks us to be his ambassadors. But to be ambassadors of Christ is not a temporary job. It's a mission that belongs to every baptized Christian. It means that at the risk of my very life I have to preach the gospel without compromise. It is in the depths of the poustinia where you have to face yourself within your own heart that you tremble. It is there that sobornost is strengthened. The pilgrimage made the bricks and now the poustinia makes the cement that holds the bricks.

You will learn what price love is, the love that Christ called all his followers to. You will have to face all the risks of that love. He said, "Greater love has no man than to lay down his life for his friends." This risk may lead even to physical death!

Perhaps the greatest risk will be sobornost! For now that you have made the pilgrimage, come to the poustinia of your heart and blending your will with God's will, you will know the pain of constant crucifixion and the joy of constant resurrection. The poustinia will make you free yourself to the deepest part, to the deepest inner part of your soul. While this is going on, Satan, who has been walking around about seeking whom he may devour, will have the power, evidently given to him by God, to tempt you. Temptations are allowed by God for the growth of our faith.

The Lord went on a pilgrimage into the desert for 40 days and he was tempted. Why shouldn't you be tempted in your poustinia? The devil is as modern as we are. Through each generation, through each decade he gathers that which can hit the hardest, and which can kick away sobornost, which can bring us all to the Tower of Babel.

Maybe at this time in our century the temptations will be psychological. Our emotions will be the stones he hurls. This is the time when you will have to enter into the realm of pure faith. That poustinia of yours which you made of your heart and offered to God must be filled with that faith!

The devil can hurl his stones but you will remember Jesus coming to Nazareth when his people wanted to stone him. The Gospel says that he made himself invisible and passed unharmed. So will you. So will I. The stones the devil hurls at us will not hit us but pass us by.

This then is the role of your inner pilgrimage and your inner poustinia which will unite you with God and teach you to unite with all your brethren. Yes, this is unity, this is sobornost.

CHAPTER 10

Becoming a Contemplative

Pilgrimage. Poustinia. Knowledge, given by God alone. Such is man's journey, or should be, from his Baptism to his death. Here again we come to the essence of Baptism, which is still quite a neglected sacrament, though coming to the fore lately, but still seemingly unknown and unsung by too many faithful, baptized people.

To be baptized in the death and resurrection of Jesus Christ is to be given the key of God's heart. It is not easy to explain this. Again the realm of faith, its dimension, the climbing, the constant climbing of the mountain of the Lord is before us. So few grasp these dimensions. So few perhaps want to enter into the mystery of it, for to be baptized in Christ and to rise up in Christ means to become a contemplative.

It is not the same thing as being a mystic as the Western Church calls some of her saints who experience strange and extraordinary phenomena. No. It is a gift of God which is part and parcel of being baptized, for now you plunge into strange, holy, mysterious waters that have become mysterious because Christ purified them. Yes, purified them by his own baptism. Now these strange, mysterious waters, and the sacrament that takes place in them for each of us faithful, transforms us. We don't come out of Baptism the way we walked into it. It makes no difference if we are just a little child, a baby in arms. No. Or a youth, an adult, or an old person. The waters of Baptism cleanse, purify, heal, beyond the understanding of man. At the moment of the immersion or when the water touches us one way or another, we become new men. Totally new!

Consider, truly consider, that out of these mysterious waters which God himself has sanctified, a child, a youth, an adult, an older person, becomes so pure, so clear, so transparent, that it isn't difficult to realize that God talks to them. Yes, but there is something else that happens. They hear God's voice. At one point or another of their life they do, just like Adam and Eve heard his voice in the breeze, in the tiny winds of eventide, when he came to talk to them. Because they hear his voice they should become contemplatives, and they do if they listen. Why? Because they have been created for this moment. They have been created to start their journey toward the heart of God. We all come from the mind of God; we all should wend our way to the heart of God. The road is very clear. It's a path. It's a way, and Christ the Son of God made it clear. "I am the way. Follow me," he said. That's what we have to do. But how can we do it unless we contemplate, that is to say, become one, for contemplation leads to total unity. Our lives are really contemplative, or should be. No matter what occupation we might be engaged in, our hearts must be made ready to be contemplative. To listen . . . to listen to God's voice and to follow it, not only to follow it, but to become one with it as time goes by.

So Baptism is truly a key to God's heart. Call it heaven if you wish to, but what is heaven except God's heart? That's heaven, and all the way to heaven is heaven if we follow Christ because he is heaven. It's so simple. So very simple.

But because we are human, because Satan is in our midst, because we are subject to emotions, fear of risks and all the other things that face us so threateningly today in our century which lacks faith, well . . . the road is somewhat divided. The Lord makes it a little easier for us to follow his path. As I said in the preceding chapter, we begin with a pilgrimage, an inward pilgrimage. Maybe we asked the blessing of our parents, but maybe we have no parents. Then we must always keep in touch with a spiritual director, for if we direct ourselves, we are total fools, and we shall not walk the path of Jesus Christ. We will forget that he alone is the way.

And so because it is so difficult to be a Christian in these days, the Lord leads us to an inward journey through which we will eventually meet the God who dwells within us and by meeting him become freer, more steadfast. But the journey inward, the pilgrimage that we must undertake, has to pass through a strange place which I call the poustinia. If your feet are firmly planted on the path of your pilgrimage—which is Jesus Christ who said, "I am the way"—then you have to pass through this house, this poustinia, this symbolic poustinia, not made of hands necessarily; the one that you are going to build in your own heart. There the path of Jesus Christ passes through you and stops for a while. There is a spot there where you can pray. You can see, if you have eyes to see, thousands of poustinias and thousands of people's knees making indentations. Yes, you have to go through the poustinia of your own heart. All of us must do so, because we have to face ourselves and meet ourselves and discard everything from ourselves that is not God's. As this is done, your doors open to everyone, for those who walk the path of Jesus Christ have always time for others. Anyhow, someday your symbolic house will vanish. There will be no isba in your heart. No place to sleep on the floor. No indentations to kneel upon. No table to read the scriptures upon as if they were food. No. Nothing will remain except love.

Quite suddenly you will realize that you are being called to another pilgrimage. A voice will come to you and say, "Come higher, friend," and you will look around. You will not believe at all that any voice came to you. It's so strange, but all this is the fruit of your Baptism. And the voice is not really a voice as the mystics talk about it. It is again a tiny breeze, very tiny, and it says, "Come on higher," and you look around you and you see that all before you is a large and high mountain and you wonder why you should go on higher, but you go higher. Remember, you are naked as Christ was naked. You have made the pilgrimage. You have gone through the poustinia. So while you walk up, up, up the mountain you wonder, and then quite suddenly you realize that it's still the way of Jesus Christ. You are still walking in his footsteps. Now it's upwards. Remember, the Lord liked to be on little hills and when he wanted to be transfigured, you remember, he took the apostles to a mountain.

Mountains, symbolically, are places from which you can see far. They offer you ever-wider horizons and now you are walking upward. The Lord will give you time to rest. There will be beautiful flower-scented, flower-filled fields. Then again his paths will lead through snowy mountains and rugged hills, but it won't matter anymore. With each step up the air is fresh and clear. You will see farther and farther. And there will be moments when you will fall upon the path of the Lord exhausted . . . torn apart: to be baptized is to follow Christ, to die and rise up with him. But don't forget the dying. Those who follow Christ must always pass through the cross and Golgotha. As soon as they do they enter into the light of the resurrection. You can see them even if you don't know them, for they are full of light, an inner light.

You fall down because the atmosphere is so clear. You move higher up, and you see. You see the disunity of people. You see the disunity of families, of children and parents, of brothers and sisters, of fellow Christians. You fall as one naked. You fall as one who is dead on the path of the Lord and you stay there without knowing why, and time will cease to exist for a while.

Then the Holy Spirit will come and overshadow you. For this he has been made an advocate, too, to rescue those who have fallen, who have followed the path of Christ, who have walked his way. He will lift you up and he will bring you anew the Spirit of the Lord. He will revive your faith, your love, your hope. You will know that you were baptized for this: to bring peace and harmony and love, faith and hope, to people, to those the Lord will allow you to meet through your life. Your feet are wedded to his way, for "I am the way." You are deep in the realization of what it means to walk naked, to walk through a poustinia still naked, but now acquiring through the Holy Spirit the gifts of wisdom, knowledge and understanding.

CHAPTER 11

Forging a Chain of Hearts

Yes, sobornost will be yours when you realize what it means to walk naked through a pilgrimage, through a poustinia, up to the mountain of the Lord. From now on you will hear the voice that calls you onto the mountain again and again. An inner voice, yet not yours. Always it will repeat the same sentence, "Friend, come on higher." This is the time when you will have to realize why sobornost took its roots in you . . . why you went through that pilgrimage . . . why you went through that poustinia, and why you are ascending the mountain of the Lord.

The answer is very simple: it is now *your* time to bring sobornost to your brethren. Yes, now is your moment to cement unity between them and yourself, remembering that God died for all people, the baptized and the unbaptized.

At the same time, very specially with great love and compassion, you will direct your whole life, your apostleship, your ambassadorship, to promote brotherhood. You have been made brothers of one another by the death of Jesus Christ and his resurrection. Now your task is before you to make that brotherhood live, to incarnate it, to bring the law of love, which is brotherhood, into the open so that people looking at all of you who are baptized will say, "Behold how those Christians love one another."

This is the task of sobornost. For this you are laying down your life as God asks you to do. For this you are undergoing martyrdom, even as our Lady underwent it. Maybe not a bloody martyrdom, but an inner martyrdom. For this you are constantly crying to God for faith, and it will continue to be until you die!

Faith alone can carry out this task of unity which the Russians call "sobornost." Nothing else will. Do you understand what type of unity I am talking about? It's a unity, total, complete, of mind, of heart, of soul. It's an inner unity that once established cannot be broken. It pertains to spiritual unity from which all the rest will follow, but it has to be first a spiritual unity.

Yes, it has to be a spiritual unity, and here we begin to understand what sobornost really means, because now it becomes palpable, visible, touchable as it grows among us who believe in Jesus Christ. Now the mysteries of his gospel are open to us. He became obedient even to death on the cross. His obedience now becomes very simple to us, for if we were of one mind with the Trinity, what else could we do but obey as he did? The Father asks him; the Son immediately agrees, and the Holy Spirit hovers over both.

The same with us. God asks us to surrender to him totally, unreservedly, without any hiding place, if we are foolish enough to think that there is a hiding place from God. Yes, that's what he asks us to do. United to the Trinity, filled with its life, and its fire and its movement, we too become creative. We create sobornost in our hearts through the grace of the Trinity.

Now we are alert, alert to the voice that says, "Friend, come higher" because that voice means very simply, "Deepen your sobornost . . . deepen it!" The time is now. Let the baptized ones be one as the Trinity is One. Deepen it. Look, the world is fragmented. People meet one another as if they were enemies, even the baptized ones! Terror reigns in the hearts of men, and fear in the hearts of children. This cannot be. It has been said of us, "See how the Christians love one another." Today it can only be said of us, "Look how these Christians hate one another."

This cannot be. We have to be united, united . . . united . . . united one with the other or we shall truly perish.

This is no time for rugged individualism. Sobornost doesn't cut out individualism where it is used in the service of God. Artists are individualists. Writers, too. All kinds of works are produced by individuals, but the spirit behind them must be one with God.

It pertains to God, you understand. It pertains to myself and God, or yourself and God.

What is your relation with God? What is my relation with God? Is it sobornost? The sobornost of total unity, obedience, joy, incarnation? Is it the understanding that we pass constantly through Golgotha, that we die with him and are resurrected with him? This isn't something that happens once to us in Baptism. It happens all the time.

But with each year, as we realize that we are brothers and sisters of one another, as we realize these tremendous verities, slowly, slowly our pilgrimage to Golgotha becomes rarer and rarer. The voice in our hearts says, "Come higher, friend," until it ceases to speak in us because we have reached the height of the mountain. Now we understand! For we see the whole panorama: the tragic life of the world and especially of the Church. All that is left to us now is to pray, for we are already at the periphery of the resurrection.

But we must pass it on to others. That's our life: to make people understand. That has to be if we are to survive . . . survive as human beings instead of beasts or bionic people. We are freed . . . freed by Christ to live a life of supernature. We don't have to wallow in the evil of our nature, especially in its animal aspects. We don't have to. We can move in freedom in the supernatural. It's our true habitat, even though it stays on the natural, for the natural is beautiful, too, once we accept it as coming from God's hands instead of somewhere else.

Yes. Listen. Listen to the wind. You are not alone. Constantly with you side by side is the Dove. See, it's the Dove that makes the wind. It's the wind of his gifts. With them we can enter the heart of another. With the gifts of love and tenderness and of the compassion of God, of Jesus Christ, we can seal the heart of another to ours as ours is sealed to God. And so begins a chain of hearts which are sealed to God and to one another. Now there is sobornost, the unity that must exist.

This unity transcends our emotions, our individualism, everything that is not itself. It transcends all things, because, you see, it is rooted in God, whereas all the other things are rooted in men. But we can gather up what is rooted in men and lift it up in a finely wrought chalice to God.

Yes, this is the task of the baptized—oneness in the Trinity. Oneness of the way that leads to the Trinity, the way of Jesus Christ who said, "I am the way." Oneness in the Holy Spirit, abundantly using his gifts for the binding of one another and all to God. And as a constant reminder, we have our Lady, the perfection of sobornost, in the unity of her heart and that of God the Father . . . and ours.

CHAPTER 12

Unity in Eucharist

Abiding in our midst is sobornost, incarnated, personified.

Yes, incarnated, personified, the person of Jesus Christ. We approach, not in fear and trembling, because he is our brother, but we take off our shoes because the place indeed is holy. Here, here, incredible as it might seem, is the sign of unity, the sign of sobornost, the sign of the gathering up, for here is the Eternal Priest. You can call him a bishop, but the words are not important. The Eternal Priest. He gathers us up. He calls us. Listen. He calls us to come, and he says, "Whoever eats my flesh and drinks my blood has eternal life, and I will raise him up on the last day" (Jn 6:54).

But these are words one has to explain because what he really means is that we will have faith in him. We shall have faith in him when we eat his body and drink his blood . . .

the very foundations of unity. It is here that the Son of Man and the Son of God brings us together around a table . . . a sobrania . . . a gathering of the faithful who believe.

"Believe." This is the operative word. You have to believe. When you come to that table, to that sobrania, to that gathering, maybe even in a sobor which is the cathedral, but that too is not important . . . wherever he is, there is the cathedral. But when we gather together around the Sacred Species, around that sacred table, in faith we see reenacted an incredible act: sacrifice and sacrament. Only faith can penetrate the depth of what transpires at that table.

The key to that table is Baptism. Always Baptism. Always death in him and resurrection in him. Only the baptized approach the mysteries and indeed the word "mysteries" is right and proper, for mysteries they are. The awesome mystery of love. The awesome mystery of unity, for this is what is happening!

This is what is happening. The Father sent his Son to redeem us—to redeem us, as we shall find in the gospel, through his death on the cross. This redemption is so overpowering, so incredible, so stupendous that men's hearts can only cry out, "Lord, I believe. Help my unbelief."

But to those of us who believe, those of us who have been wedded through sobornost with the heart of the Trinity, faith has been given in Baptism. Now the fulness of Baptism is ours, for we have understood that it is through Baptism that we have this fantastic faith, this incredible faith to believe that Jesus is with us always, and the strange, incredible fact also that daily or weekly, as the case may be, in the East or the West, we might partake of the Most Holy Species—the bread and the wine.

Now we stand purified before this awesome sacrament. Baptism took away our sins when we were immersed in the holy waters. The sacrament of the Eucharist washes our sins away, for we come to it no matter how holy we may be, with the dust of the world upon our holiness. Few of us are really holy but the sacrament of the Eucharist itself takes away our sins. True, some of the sins we have to confess, but if there is contrition the sacrament of the Eucharist will wash the dust away. Yes, it will.

Behold the cleansing of the lepers. The lepers that are cleansed by the most holy sacrament of the Eucharist become one. The baptized ones who become one are shiny, and from their hearts the praise to God rises like a thousand songs, for they have been freed once again. Once again they have gone through the death of Christ and into his resurrection.

But there is another aspect to the most holy sacrament of the Eucharist. Incredible as it might seem, you and I have the strength of God, for God is in us and he has said, "Amen, amen, I say to you, he who believes in me, the works that I do he also shall do, and greater than these he shall do. . ." (Jn 14:12). Now the road to sobornost is yours for you are penetrated with God. Now nothing is impossible to the prayer of faith, and to you. Now sobornost becomes a reality. It is truly clothed with flesh—the flesh of Jesus Christ. Yes, the most holy sacrament of the Eucharist penetrates the faithful beyond our ken. Now we stride across mountains like gazelles, following our Beloved, and mountains become our habitat. Nothing can stop us. The most holy sacrament of the Eucharist brings sobornost in such a fashion that we must thank God and praise him for it.

Listen well, "Let him kiss me with the kiss of his mouth"

(Sg 1:2). Not only does he become one in me, but he kisses me. Go deeper, friend, and understand the sobornost that binds us through the most holy sacrament of the Eucharist. The Bridegroom comes. Hear him? He leaps over the mountains like a gazelle. Yes, the Bridegroom comes. Sobornost becomes the breath of the Lover, the Beloved.

The mysteries of the sacrament of the Holy Eucharist are high and deep, high and wide. He will reveal them to each of us within the enclosed garden of his love.

There is no way to clarify this aspect of sobornost except to fall flat on our faces upon having received the Most Holy Species and his kiss, and lay prostrate before the Unity that God the Father has sent us, for the sign of that unity and its substance is Jesus Christ.

CHAPTER 13

Service in Christ

When we consider the most holy sacrament of the Eucharist, its infinite mysteries and the infinite love of God which is enclosed in it, there is nothing left for us to do but prostrate ourselves in adoration in total faith.

To prostrate oneself before God is right and proper for we are his creatures and he is the creator and prostration is a natural act before him who is!

But we cannot remain prostrate for the simple reason that the Lord Jesus Christ became incarnate and announced loudly and clearly that the faithful had two tasks to fulfill in their lives, and Baptism, as always, was the key to the tasks. He said, "Pray always," and he said, "I have come to serve"!

We have discussed the approach to sobornost, an approach of prayer one might say, the approach of contemplation. Now Baptism, prayer, contemplation, pilgrimage, poustinia and the ascent of the mountain must become real. Now we must show the world the reality of Christ. The only way to show the world the reality of Christ is to become an icon of Christ, or a reflection of his face, and the reflection of his face will make us serve; not only pray, but serve. The two go together. There is no service without prayer, and no prayer without service for those who follow Christ. They pray always and they serve always. So now we have to enter the world, not the world that God condemned which is evil, but the world that he created . . . the beautiful world. We have to restore it.

The restoration of the world—strangely enough, the very word means rest: *rest-ora* (prayer)-*tion* (action), prayer and action. To rest at the feet of the Trinity, to contemplate him, to pray to him, is good. But then one has to take the whole word "restoration" and understand that you and I have to walk under its banner into that world that has been twisted out of shape, polluted, and made unrecognizable from what God wanted it to be. Now the task is ours.

But we cannot—we never can—decide to restore the world according to our own mind. No, no, no! If each one of us is going to decide how the world should be restored, the resulting mess would make the Tower of Babel look like a kindergarten.

Service must be service in Christ. We must act as Christ would act. We must ask ourselves each time—what would Christ do if he were I? The Gospels will tell us. We will have to follow him without compromise. There will be no possibility of any kind of prevarication or rationalization.

To serve mankind, to restore mankind to what it was in the mind of God when he created it, this is our task, for we have been baptized. Remember? We have died with Christ and we have been resurrected and if we listen carefully, the gospel will shout at us clearly and simply—not only talk to us, but shout at us—and we will have to do what it says.

That will be service—to live and preach the gospel without compromise because we want to be united with the Trinity, with the Son of God and the Son of Man who came to redeem us, with the Advocate who is supposed to lead us and is leading us into the right direction of this service that God demands. Now we are faced with the reality of sobornost.

It is not enough to contemplate, to be in ecstasy before him. It will do us no good. Ecstasies will disappear and the contemplation will vanish, and God will veil his face because we have not done what his Son has come to tell us to do. No, we have to put ourselves into the risk of following Christ to the end. We have to activate this risk, and the pain that is concomitant with it, to make it visible, touchable, possible, for mankind today is hopeless, or almost.

Consider the loneliness, the alienation, the fragmentation of all unity: the unity of husband and wife, the unity of children and parents, of children among themselves, the unity of governments and their peoples, economic unity which is nonexistent because it is not based on the gospel teachings of Christ.

The gospel has to be lived without compromise and thereby it gives hope. But today all is under the vicious hands of Satan. Men have gone up on a certain mountain, but not that of the Lord. They have listened . . . they have adored, and they have received what Satan promised: wealth for some, hunger for wealth for others, for through their hunger for wealth even the poor have been polluted by Satan, torn away from the gospel because they want to be rich.

Behold, see how long is the list of people who desire to

climb on everybody else's shoulders so as to acquire this wealth they hunger for. We call it a "mobile society." Maybe it's mobile . . maybe it's moving, but it's moving downward, not upward. It's an excrement and not a society. There is so little compassion in that society. Each wants his pound of flesh and doesn't care where he gets it. Its economics is bound to what we call today "multinational corporations." The silver passes hands from one person to another. Governments are not immune. Members of the government are not immune. Even the President of the United States is not immune to the silver. Could it be 30 pieces again?

If it isn't gold or silver they desire, it's power. Where is the gospel of humility, of simplicity and directness? Tell me. Tell me. You who read these lines, tell me!

Economics . . . politics . . . slowly, slowly, as I said so many years ago in my book, *Friendship House,* the net of the devil falls. It is not the net that Christ meant when he said, "Cast your net." The apostles did so in faith and got a hundred fish or more. No. This is a different net. It catches and it binds. Men cannot live anymore like this because, you see, in that net hope is dying!

But it isn't dead because the believers, those who are true to their Baptism, who have partaken of the most holy sacrament of the Eucharist, have cried out, "Out of the depths I cry to you, O Lord, help me! Have mercy on us!" He heard our cry. He helped us and he came through his incarnation, his death and resurrection. He brought sobornost in its full reality and a completeness that mankind had never known before.

It is so simple. Those who decided to practice the gospel without compromise, to accept the risk of following Christ, have brought hope. They who have become poor for his sake are wealthy beyond measure, for they can give what he has given to them. "I have no silver or gold," said Peter, but he cured someone. This is exactly what the baptized do who believe, who cry out, who follow, who are ready to restore the world to Christ, to his Father, to the Trinity, at whatever price they have to pay for it.

That is exactly why they bring hope, for they bring healing, help. It flows from them to whoever touches them or comes in contact with them. Soon people realize that the baptized ones who believe with their whole soul, body, mind, with everything they have, in Jesus Christ, and believe that they have to serve in the everyday little things of this world, but also in big things—politics, economics, labor, peace—are the harbingers of hope. Yes, those who come in contact with them know very soon that they are not strangers. The baptized ones know no strangers; they only know brotherhood. Their hands are always open to hold the hands of another. They form like a chain and together they walk into the darkness, the darkness created by Satan. They are not afraid, you see, because they walk in prayer and they walk to serve. They are not afraid because they walk in the shadow of the Lord. He walks ahead of them, the harbinger of hope himself. His shadow falls over the faithful, and where there is darkness there comes light, and slowly Satan retreats as he retreated in the desert.

Yes, those who believe, those who realize what Baptism is, and what the most holy sacrament of the Eucharist is, and what the incarnation means . . . fire . . . service . . . prayer . . . are true heirs of the Father.

Through service we become brothers of him who came

to serve. So hope walks again, for those who understand sobornost do not quarrel among themselves. They are not divisive because division serves Satan beautifully and kills hope easily. They know now that they have to hold one another's hands. They know now that they have to think alike, as their brother Jesus Christ thinks, otherwise their strength dwindles. There is no divisiveness among those who understand what it is all about.

They are not all alike. There is diversity in them because the Lord wants to have a garden full of diversity . . . no two people alike. He probably threw the mold away. But in that great diversity there is a vast unity that follows Christ without compromise, loving God, loving themselves, loving each other, loving everybody they come across, especially their enemies, ready to lay their life down even as Christ did.

They enter the field of economics, of politics, of marriage, of human relations. There is not a realm of man's behavior, and of man's work, that the baptized ones who love God, who partake of his Body and Blood and who understand the incarnation, prayer and service, do not make their own.

The only way to bring hope is to sharpen the lance and dig it deep into one's own heart, thus making a door for everybody to go through to Christ because sometimes the face of Christ is so obscure that your face must stand between him and the other. That's when the lance enters, to take the other by the hand and say, "I am a door to the way," and you can make them come into your wound of love. Going through the wound of love they are resurrected in hope and see the face of Christ . . . compassionate, gentle, saying, "All things are possible to those who believe in me."

CHAPTER 14

The Little Mandate

Yes, faith, love and hope give those who are one with Christ the strength to sharpen the lance of love, the lance that will pierce their own heart and make a door to God for those who seek him. Those who seek him will meet him. And when they meet him, his gentle and compassionate face will bend over them, and his quiet voice will say, "All things are possible to those who believe in me."

This chapter will have to be a somewhat personal one, personal not only to me but also to the apostolate of Madonna House. To begin with I am Russian. For many years I have tried to bring East and West together—because I love the East and the West so tremendously and because I desired from childhood to witness the greatest sobornost, that is, the immense unity of the Catholic Church and of the Orthodox Church become a reality in our world. A real sobornost that men could touch and see, a sobornost that would overcome old hurts and old ways. Yes, for this I have prayed all my life—reechoing the voice of Christ who said, "That all of them may be one, Father, just as you are in me and I am in you" (Jn 17:21).

At one point in this life of mine when I seemed to have become very comfortable, shall we say, earning a good salary, having a lovely apartment in New York, the Holy Spirit began his work upon my soul. I have to acknowledge this, and I think that this is the place to do so.

In me, a stranger in a manner of speaking, and I could say a lonely stranger, sobornost was growing and I wanted to dedicate my life to the gospel without compromise, for I didn't see any other way in which one person, all alone, very unimportant, Russian to boot, in an American society or a Canadian one, could possibly bring Christ to those whom God allowed her to meet.

But it was not easy because I had commitments and also I had finally arrived at some financial security. Somehow the Holy Spirit pursued me. I used to go lecturing far abroad, in the United States and in Canada. I also managed lecturers. A strange situation took place. Traveling in cars or boats or trains to the tune of the wheels I would hear snatches, very powerful snatches of sentences, that were relevant to me and to the gospel.

I used to write them down on pieces of paper or envelopes or what-have-you. One day I upended three or four purses—summer and winter ones. I saw a lot of pieces of envelopes and paper, even scraps of wrapping paper torn from one parcel or another. So I sat down—it was evening—and I decided I must put order in this chaos. I did, and this is what came forth:

Arise—go! Sell all you possess . . . give it directly, personally to the poor. Take up My cross (their cross) and follow Me—going to the poor—being poor—being one with them—one with Me.

Little—be always little . . . simple—poor—childlike.

Preach the Gospel WITH YOUR LIFE—WITHOUT COMPROMISE—listen to the Spirit—He will lead you.

Do little things exceedingly well for love of Me.

Love—love—love, never counting the cost.

Go into the marketplace and stay with Me . . . pray . . . fast . . . pray always . . . fast.

Be hidden—be a light to your neighbor's feet. Go without fears into the depth of men's hearts . . . I shall be with you.

Pray always, I WILL BE YOUR REST.

When I looked at it I got frightened. Perhaps the word is not "frightened," but "awed." Here, with unmistakable clarity, the light of the Holy Spirit fell on the path of Jesus Christ, on his way that I had followed, as far as I knew, but when I saw it in this light, this fantastic light that seemed to stream from nowhere, I decided that it certainly was an illusion.

However, I also decided to check this. I often opened the bible at random, and always my eyes fell on the words, "If thou wilt be perfect, go, sell your possessions and give to the poor, and you will have treasure in heaven. Then come, follow me." Not trusting my bibles—I had a few—I even went to the public library, got a rather huge bible, opened it at random, and what did I read? "Go, sell your possessions and give to the poor, and you will have treasure in heaven. Then come, follow me."

At this point I sought the advice of priests because these bible coincidences were too much for me. Each one told me that I had deep commitments and I should keep them. One commitment was a child. I understood this, and I tried my level best to obey those priests.

But I had no peace. The Holy Spirit was truly over-shadowing me and I could hear the beating of his wings, if you want to put it that way.

I don't know if you have ever heard the beating of the wings of the Holy Spirit. It's a most powerful sound. It comes as a wind, but not a gentle wind. It comes as a fierce wind. It blows away all preconceived notions and all confusion from your heart as well as your mind. Everything disappears that man relies on. It seems as if this wind of the Holy Spirit folds the wings of the intellect, and the intellect rests. Everything is suspended. Suddenly a dimension of God which you never knew existed is revealed to you. You understand that indeed you have to arise and go. You have to arise and go and fulfill not only the first paragraph, but all the rest of the Little Mandate that you had written so simply and unsuspectingly on little bits of paper!

I have been used to obedience from childhood. I would not undertake such a thing on my own. I would consider even the Holy Spirit an illusion, if it were not confirmed by either a spiritual director or by the bishop of my diocese, for I firmly believe, as my father told me, that the bishop is the "custodian of my soul."

In Russia sobornost is the bishop. He is also the sobor from which sobornost stems. Sobor means Cathedral, the bishop's church, as I have already explained. But the bishop himself is a sobor because where he is unity should be. In his very person he connects the faithful to God and God to them. He is the center. He is the one ordained and he passes this ordination on to his priests. I had to ask my bishop if this Little Mandate which appeared to be from the Holy Spirit was of the Holy Spirit. He alone could say yes or no.

So believing as I do, to the bishop I went, to the archbishop of my diocese I went, and I laid before him all that was on my soul. I showed him the Little Mandate crudely typed. I told him that I wished to sell all that I possessed, that I wished to go into the poustinia of the marketplace. He did not quite understand what a poustinia was, but as I explained it, it became clear to him. He was that kind of archbishop. He gave me leeway to follow what he considered to be truly the promptings of the Holy Spirit. But he said that I should spend a year thinking and praying about it; which I did.

So one day, when the year ended (dates are not important to me, nothing is very important that is not of God)— I sold all that I possessed and I went to the slums of a fairly large city, there to live in prayer and service, to pray and to serve where I was needed.

I thought of it as Nazareth where the Lord prayed always and served. Oh, he must have made lovely chairs and tables for young people who were getting married, cradles for babies and so forth. Perhaps I was a little young, but I thought of my vocation in a very simple way. I certainly did not want to start anything, least of all an organization, a community, or a lay apostolate. I wanted to pray and serve *by myself* according to this Little Mandate and the ways of my people.

Why do I call these scribblings of mine written on bits of paper and which I wrote out one day in a consecutive way, why do I call them a Little Mandate? Because it truly is my mandate from God to preach the gospel without compromise.

This whole Mandate is filled with the Trinity, with the Father, the Son and the Holy Spirit, and with Our Lady of the Trinity. It breathes union between God and mankind. It is replete with sobornost.

It is of it that I want to talk now.

This Mandate now belongs to Madonna House since the Lord changed my original vocation of praying and serving the people by myself in the poustinia of the marketplace to become the foundress of a lay apostolate. Truly the ways of God are unsearchable!

So the Little Mandate became the charter of Friendship House first and then of Madonna House. Today we take vows of poverty, chastity and obedience according to this Mandate to preach the gospel with our lives all the better.

However, as you will see, this Mandate can be lived by anyone because it has its roots in the gospel which is the property of every baptized person.

Now back to Madonna House. Let's look. What do the members of Madonna House bind themselves to when they accept the Little Mandate? First and foremost, they agree to arise and leave all that they possess. They begin the journey inward that is undertaken to meet the God who dwells within. For this all possessions are left aside.

Of course, in Madonna House it means a true dispossession, or it should, of all material wealth. Poverty, according to Paul Evdokimov, a celebrated Russian theologian, means "when the need to have becomes the need not to have." Meditate on that sentence—that lovely Russian sentence, though of course it belongs to the early monastic life of all peoples, but still it's very Russian.

But it becomes also yours. You, too, are called to poverty as all baptized faithful are. Some who read *Sobornost* will become naked, but there will be few called to this total nakedness.

But "sharing the wealth" should become simplicity itself to all. For your love of Christ, the Holy Spirit, the grace of the Father, will tell your conscience how far you have to go to share the wealth. No two people are the same as to sharing the wealth, but all who believe in Jesus Christ should be "dispossessed" . . . by not being attached to anything except the Most Holy Trinity.

Let's go down a little further. Here in the Little Mandate it says, "Little—be always little . . . simple—poor—childlike." This eschews arrogance, the arrogance of the intellect which is so prevalent in the West. Everything has to be according to the way I think it has to be. And so economics, politics, peace, war—all are shot around about, and divisiveness is endless everywhere. Especially in the last decades this divisiveness entered the heart of religious orders, both female and male, entered into the priesthood, the diocese. It enters into the family. It enters into the children.

Listen. Can you hear the breakup of the world? The pollution extends not only into the earth and the river and the air, but the heart itself of mankind is in danger of being totally polluted. It ceases to be little. It ceases to be childlike. It ceases to be simple and it ceases to be poor. As a result, listen again to the cacophony of voices which come falling from the lips of Satan slaying people all over the world, leaving them as dead, hungry and cold and alone. Suicide rates mount because man has ceased to be little, to be simple, to be childlike.

Let's go on and take the third paragraph of the Little Mandate of Madonna House. It says, "Peach the Gospel with your life—without compromise—listen to the Spirit—He will lead you."

Yes, the time has come for Madonna House and for all of you who believe in Jesus Christ, and who hunger for him and for that unity which he alone can bring to bear against divisiveness . . . yes, the time has come for all to have the courage to submit your intellect to that of Jesus Christ as he operates in your family, in your personal relations, in governments, Madonna House, religious orders, everything, everywhere. Arrogance has no place when we desire to preach the Gospel without compromise, because he who is the gospel said, "Learn of me for I am meek and humble of heart."

The Little Mandate continues: "Do little things exceedingly well for love of Me." Like a whisper that ruffles the trees at night, in the same breeze the Lord comes to us and repeats this fourth paragraph of the Mandate. Can you hear the voice of the leaves that gently, even as God is gentle to you, say, "I don't ask for big things. I ask for little things done well for the loved one."

Here I repeat again the incarnation comes to greet you, for isn't that what he did . . . little things, exceedingly well, for love of us? Can you visualize a table or chair that was not perfect when it left his hands? He did everything well for the love of his Father . . . for the love of us. He gave us the example: "Do little things exceedingly well for the love of Me."

And so he reduced love to our size. We are little people.

His immense love, as we read about it in the scriptures, over-powers us, but as we listen to the leaves in the evening and hear his voice come gently and simply saying "Do little things exceedingly well for love of Me," the housework begins to be a way of loving him.

The way of loving him is very simple: the diapers, the baking, the laundry, the sitting quietly telling stories to her children, and holding the hand of her husband. All are little acts of love, directed not only to a woman's family but to God. This is what he wants. The farmer ploughing his field, the farmwife churning her butter, realize that this is what he asks. The stenographer who is in love with God knows that the letters she types perfectly, or with two fingers, are acts of love. The nurse, the taxidriver, everyone everywhere can absorb this fourth paragraph of the Little Mandate. So simple. So easy. It's a song of love.

Listen to the dishes. Listen to the laundry. Listen to the work of the gardener . . . the farmer. A great and beautiful chorus is lifting itself up from the hearts of men who believe. And the love of Jesus Christ responds to that chorus of love because that's the way he worked for many years, writing us love letters.

Listen! He started writing us love letters from the moment he was born. This is what we are talking about. The first cry of the Infant at Christmas was a love letter of God to man. A tiny little thing. Just the squalling of a baby. Yes. And then, when he was little, he tried to imitate Joseph and hammered at all kinds of things. Can you hear hammering? It's another love letter of the little Christ to us. Then the measured hammering of a competent carpenter. Another love letter.

Little things done exceedingly well for the love of him.

He showed us the way of those little things for the love of us.

Then they became big things. For the next love letter we heard was the sound of leather on a man's back—his flagellation. The next love letter we heard was the hammering of nails on soft flesh.

The last love letter came from the cross: "This is your mother."

All little things. Seemingly unimportant, but oh, how vastly important because to Madonna House members this is part of their living the gospel without compromise. But it's yours, too, for the taking.

Then comes: "Love—love—love, never counting the cost." Well, there is very little that I can say about that. The world is a very cold place these days because people do not love. There is lust. There is temporary commitment to what appears to be love but it is not lasting enough to be called love. Love is stronger than death.

Love is a Person. Because love is God, that's why love is stronger than death. Meditate on it. Contemplate it. You will begin to understand the source of true love, the heart of God.

Now comes the next paragraph, "Go into the market-place and stay with me . . . pray . . . fast . . . pray always . . . fast." Yes, these days what my father used to say really must take place. He used to say, "If you want to reach God you must lift two arms, fasting and prayer."

In our days when everybody is catering to the appetites of the flesh, in our days when senses rule as if they were God, it is time that we should fast as well as pray.

The Lord fasted quite a bit and we should follow his footsteps. He said to his apostles when they complained that they couldn't cast the devil out from someone, "This kind can be cast out in no way except by prayer and fasting" (Mk 9:28).

We who are of one mind and one heart, who have held hands to walk into the darkness of this world to restore it, we must continue to do so in the marketplace and stay in that marketplace and fast and pray.

Then that Little Mandate tells us, "Be hidden—be a light to your neighbor's feet. Go without fears into the depth of men's hearts . . . I shall be with you." It ends by saying, "Pray always. I will be your rest."

The last sentence is the consoling one, but here we have to come to a strange sentence: *Be hidden*. All of us have to carry the cross of the Lord. There isn't anyone in Madonna House or outside of it among Christians who could possibly be without a cross.

It's through the cross that we reach the resurrection. We should be absolutely sure of this truth, and we should keep this cross hidden and not place it on the shoulders of others. It is our cross we have to carry. It is the one God has given us to go through into his resurrection. This is the one we should keep hidden.

But there are crosses and crosses, some of our own making. These we should immediately discard. Some permitted by God for our sanctification. These we can share for they are also for the sanctification of others. True, we can help to carry other people's crosses and they can help to carry our crosses, but the operative word is "hidden."

The Lord said, "So when you give to the needy, do not announce it with trumpets as the hypocrites do in the synagogues and on the streets, to be honored by men," and "When you fast, put oil on your head and wash your face, so that it will not be obvious to men that you are fasting, but only to your Father, who is unseen; and your Father, who sees what is done in secret, will reward you" (Mt 6:16-18).

Our very hiddenness becomes a light if we do not complain, if we carry our cross manfully, ready to help in the carrying of other people's crosses. Then we become a light to our neighbor's feet because we become an icon of Christ—shining!

Then we go without fear into men's hearts because we know God will lead us to them—to those hearts, because we know that he wants us to be there, because he will be our rest and he will teach us to pray always in that heart.

But this is only possible if we are one with him, if there is no divisiveness among us, if we are of one mind. For then indeed we are hidden and we are revealed as the men and women that we should be: men who pray for peace and are peaceful, men who pray for unity and are united, men who pray for sobornost and are a sobornost.

CHAPTER 15

Obstacles to Sobornost

We have to face many things before this reality of sobornost can become incarnate in the heart of modern men. But a flashback to the beginning and then a return to our days will show us that very little has changed over a period of thousands of years.

What are the obstacles to unity, to sobornost? Well, they begin in a garden, maybe a totally symbolic garden—it's not very important—but a garden is a good place to begin. God walked in it and talked with men. They heard his voice and he gave them what we call commandments, but they were phrased so gently.

He taught them to do many things: to name the beasts, the flowers, the grains. He gave them the earth to cherish— to work it and to cherish it. And he told them to multiply. Then he allowed them to eat of all the fruits of the land except the fruit of a certain tree, because he knew that it would separate them from him and shatter the sobornost which existed between him and them.

But they ate it and thus they disobeyed the gentle voice that had spoken to them while God walked in the garden with them.

Yes, they disobeyed, and at that moment the unity between themselves and God was severed, the sobornost fragmented, yet not without hope. God gave them hope. Even while they were leaving paradise he was worried about their covering. He wanted them to have warm clothing. So there was hope and they left this symbolic paradise with his love, with hope, and with faith that someday that strange darkness that had become theirs because of eating the fruit would disperse.

The wound of disobedience was transmitted to their children and their children's children, and it came to us. Notwithstanding the fact that God sent his Son to heal that wound of original sin, to wash it away by his death on the cross and his resurrection, its effects still remain with us. We continue to eat the fruit. We continue to disobey.

Behold! Look around. See? The fruit of the tree of the poor man's garden is quickly plucked by the hands of the rich man who not only wants the fruit tree, but the earth on which it grows and the house of the poor man and all that belongs to him.

All over the world people are eating of the forbidden fruit . . . the fruit of arrogance, of pride, of avarice, the rich nations robbing the poor nations, the wealthy pushing the poor into the dust and trampling on them. And so disobedience to the Lord grows and the gospel is not preached without compromise. In fact, it is barely preached at all, among the Christians, anyway. The rich rationalize it away and the poor are unable to hear it because of their hunger. And my soul cries out to God, "Give bread to the hungry and hunger for you to those who have bread!"

So the first obstacle to unity is disobedience. The second one is pride. Again, perhaps, we have to call it "arrogance" but maybe "pride" will be the best word. When men decided to be like God and built themselves a tower they called Babel so that they, in their ignorance, could reach God, that was the day when God divided men by languages, when sobornost and pride lay in the dust. God still could talk to man, but they couldn't talk to one another. Sobornost demands that God talk to men, that men listen to God and, turning around to their fellowmen and brothers in Christ, pass on what God told them as well as pass on to God what men told one another.

Yes, sobornost and pride lay in the dust, but not for long. Pride reared itself up, shook the dust away and proceeded to walk through the centuries. It is with us now. Sobornost humbly stayed behind.

Governments talk about sovereignty. But sovereignty, as understood today, is selfishness, arrogance and pride. It refuses to love, to share, to give hope and faith. It is the pride that shook the dust of centuries from itself to walk among us as if man really adored himself.

That sovereignty left the footstool of God and sold itself to Satan, becoming pride—a pride that holds nations enslaved. Pride that sits on a bunch of bags filled with gold. Pride whose other names today are selfishness, terrorism, torture.

Yes, it is among us not only an inheritance from the old pagan days of Babylon, Assyria, Egypt, but from our contemporaries, Stalin, Hitler, Mussolini. That sort of pride that wants to be like God is death to sobornost, to unity with God.

How stupid is man! He doesn't understand as Paul Evdokimov says, that if we abolish the face of God we abolish the face of man.

Yes, these are the great obstacles against the unity of men with God and so against sobornost. But there is an obstacle that lives among all of us like mice do, like cockroaches, so much so that that we get used to it and it gnaws at our brain in little bits, like mice do on a piece of cheese.

You might think that the great obstacle to unity, to sobornost is atheistic communism, and so it is, but this is no cheese for little mice to gnaw at. This is for lions and tigers to tear apart.

No. The real obstacle to sobornost lies in the hearts, lies in the minds of all Christians *who have not understood or who have forgotten what it means to be baptized.*

Often under the guise of true Christianity people set themselves to break sobornost. They do it very simply by rationalizing Christ's teachings, selecting that part only which satisfies their minds and hearts. Obedience is not in them; it is neither their forte nor their desire. They have forgotten the Christ who was obedient unto death, even the death of the cross. And so they tear his teachings apart.

But the strange thing is that it does not make them free. The more ruthless their preaching becomes, the more vivid their speech, the more aggressive their utterances, the less can they rest. For they follow their own will; they do not follow God's will.

Those who follow their own will are cut off from God, from his Mystical Body, and from the People of God. They stand alone, prey not only to their own will, but to Satan's endless whispers.

Yes, this is the great obstacle to unity: when the mind of man challenges the mind of God, refusing obedience, refusing submission, refusing entry into the reality which is Christ.

This is the most painful, the most tragic picture that exists today in our century, in our decade, now unrolling before our eyes: *man worshipping himself*. Man saying loudly and clearly, "I am the master of my destiny. I can solve all the problems of my life."

Oh, some will yet acknowledge that in moments of grave difficulty, of tremendous crossroads, they might turn their faces to God and ask him his advice almost as if they were equal. Others simply deny there is a God. And others, beholding the modern scene, are almost afraid to move, to put out their hand to grasp the hand of another so as together to be able to hold on to the hand of God which means unity, sobornost, peace in the midst of turmoil.

Yes, divisiveness from the will of God is the saw in the hands of Satan that can cut man's unity with God by even, perhaps, cutting man's hand off.

Strange when you look at the Little Mandate how the words can suddenly be turned round about by the hands of Satan. Satan is an empty shell, you know. He can only use and pervert that which comes from the lips of God. This is his forte. So he takes the Little Mandate which came to Madonna House and is open to all of you, and twists it around.

He whispers as he whispered once upon a time to a

woman, "Take the fruit and eat it. You will know good from evil." So he whispers now in our day, "Oh, you don't have to do big things. Nobody asks you to be a rebel. No. Just get together with one or two people. Cast a little darkness about this or that with one or two people. Start a little gossip about this or about that, a priest, a superior, a wife, a husband, children, an office girl, a nurse. Just a little gossip. Tell them about how difficult those bosses are. How impatient. How unjust, especially to yourself. How intolerant the wife or the husband is; how sloppy that nurse is and how ungrateful the children. Spread the rumors."

The communists know that technique very well. So did the Romans when they ruled by division (*Divide et impera*). The communists apply it now to other people everywhere, and little things are done exceedingly well at the instigation of Satan.

Yes. What are the obstacles to unity?

—Disobedience to God, severing your sobornost and his.

—Pride, arrogance, avarice, greed, breaking sobornost between peoples, governments, all kinds of bodies of men and women, unions, employers, families, etc.

—The Tower of Babel that so many men build into their hearts wanting to be like God.

—And finally the fantastic ability of the devil to use the words of God to further his growth—little things done very well at his bidding.

These are the Damoclean swords that hang over man united to God.

CHAPTER 16

We Have a Father

"He who sees me sees my Father," said Jesus Christ. Later he promised his disciples that he would not leave them orphans. He said, "I will send to you from the Father, the Spirit of truth who goes out from the Father. . ." (Jn 15:26). So out of the words of Jesus Christ himself we "get a glimpse" of the Trinity.

Here we have such a glimpse that it truly makes man reel with joy, or should.

Consider. Consider everyday life: you who are lonely, you who are seeking love, you who feel rejected, you who feel neglected, you who feel like orphans even if you have parents, you who feel alienated from society and from your family . . . stop, stop for one moment and try, try, just try to meditate on the words of Jesus Christ.

He tells us we have a Father. He says that who sees him

sees the Father. And when the apostles asked him how to pray he gave them these beautiful words: "Our Father who art in heaven. . . ." Do you hear that? Does your heart listen? "Our Father who art in heaven. . . ." We have a Father. "Abba." We are not alienated, we are not abandoned, we are not orphans, we are not rejected. . . . None of these things really happens to us simply because we do have a Father. "Our Father who art in heaven, hallowed be thy name. Thy kingdom come. Thy will be done on earth as it is in heaven. Give us this day our daily bread, and forgive us our trespasses as we forgive those who trespass against us. Lead us not into temptation but deliver us from evil."

Look at it. Listen to it. Write it out. Savor every word. We have a Father. How beautiful! How wonderful! All the strength that belongs to a father, or should, is in him whom we call "Our Father."

Yes, we have a Father, but we also have a Brother, and they are so united, there is such a sobornost between them. And he who sees the Son sees the face of the Father. Jesus Christ was not content to leave some kind of fantastic picture of a man with a big beard. No. He told them, "Listen. Listen with your heart. Listen with your joy. Listen with your gladness. Listen with your sorrow. He who sees me sees the Father."

We have a concrete picture of the Father. True, we haven't seen Christ. You and I haven't seen Christ. But others, others who lived in his time have seen him. They have looked at his face and those who believed . . . those who believed knew that the face of the Father was reflected in the Son.

Is it a double image? I don't think so, and yet it might be. The mysteries of the Trinity are of such depth that no one can plumb them. I think that the icon of the Father is reflected in the icon of the Son: the face of the Father in the face of the Son. In faith let us understand that clearly, for when we even mention the word "Trinity" we are entering the realm of faith. It might be dark for us, but not if we humbly rest before it, not trying to fathom it any further than what Christ said, "He who sees me sees my Father."

In the quiet of our rest, let us slowly, taking days, not minutes, not hours, but days to recite this glorious prayer, "Our Father who art in heaven. . . ." We could spend a year or two on just that one sentence.

If the hands of your heart are folded on the lap of your heart . . . if your intellect has closed its wings, and if you are at rest . . . the rest that only God can give . . . then much of the mystery of the Trinity that the Lord desires to reveal to you will be revealed to you in various ways. But all the time you will know that you have a Father and that will change your life.

Yes, you have a Father who is in heaven. You have a Brother, Jesus Christ, whom the Father sent to redeem us . . . to redeem us unto the death on the cross. Oh blessed cross through which I have to pass to be always and forever in the resurrected Christ!

It is then that the Holy Spirit, promised by Father and Son, will make his appearance. Various people have seen him in the shape of a dove. He is so spoken of in the Gospels. Some of the Russians call him "the Crimson Dove, the God of Love," for that is who he is. Three in One, or One in Three, God is Love. The Advocate, the Promised One.

How afraid they must have been when he ascended. Oh yes, he promised not to leave them orphans, but they did not understand. So many times they did not understand, nor do we. So many times he speaks in our hearts and we discard his soft voice. It does not jive with our brilliant technologically trained intellect, so we either miss it or discard it.

Well, the apostles believed.

But who was this Advocate? Who was this strange person who wouldn't leave them orphans after he who was their whole life had left? They couldn't understand. So for 10 days they cringed at the feet of our Lady in the upper room. "Cringed" is the word. They were afraid of the Sanhedrin; they were afraid of the Pharisees and the Sadducees, of the Romans—everybody in authority. They were afraid of their own Jews. So they cringed. But there was one good thing about that cringing: they prayed with her. One day—we call it "Pentecost"—the day of the Spirit, they heard the roaring of a great wind.

Did it ever occur to you that God has often come in the wind? He talked to Adam and Eve in the soft breeze of evening. He came to Elijah who expected him to come roaring like thunder also in a gentle wind. And if you listen well, my friends, he will come to you, usually in a gentle wind.

But this time he didn't. No. This time the wind was roaring indeed. It shook the place. Their fears for a moment, for a second, grew. But then out of the wind came fire! Yes, out of the wind came fire . . . tongues of fire . . . and they rested upon the heads of the apostles, and of our Lady, too. The Promised One had arrived, the Third Person of the Most Holy Trinity!

Bow down your head. Prostrate yourself, for the place is beyond holiness. God came to man in tongues of fire! The word "holy" ceases to apply.

Once more man, did he know it or not, beheld heaven, for heaven is Love, and Love is God!

The Promised One had come . . . he whom Jesus Christ called "the Advocate." Advocate? In French *avocat*. But in Russian, as in other languages, the word is "Paraclete," "Consoler."

Well, an advocate pleads before a judge, and it is hoped consoles the one for whom he pleads. But in the East the thought is simply "Consoler."

The Father, the Brother, the Consoler. Just think of that. Think, you who, I repeat, are lonely. Don't be lonely. You have a Father. You have a Brother. You have a Consoler. Moreover, you have a Mother—our Lady of the Most Holy Trinity!

Once again I repeat, ignorant as I am of mysteries, but I did lay my hands in the lap of my heart, and I did listen, and I did not try to penetrate any mystery of God with my intellect. It was truly folded before them. In his infinite mercy, gently, and I am sure in a minimum quantity, for I was too poor to be given maximum quantities, the Lord spoke to me as he will speak to you if you close the wings of your intellect, put your folded hands in your open heart, and rest in him, allowing him to tell you that which he wishes to tell you—not that which you desire to know. For once you are in that state of rest, all desires disappear except the desire for the Desired One.

Yes, so I think of our Lady as being in the midst of the Trinity. I said once that if I use my imagination, which I seldom do, I think of the Trinity as movement, fire and peace. In that eternal peace she who is the spouse of the Holy Spirit, the mother of Jesus Christ, and the daughter of the Father, obviously, so it seems to me, must be in their midst.

But I have no words that can cover this picture. What is the word "in their midst" when the Lord, the Most Holy Trinity, embraces not only our poor little planet but all the spheres and galaxies and constellations? The dark void is no void to the Trinity. All is light, because all is embraced by him.

So when I say "in the midst," we are really all in the midst of the Trinity, for we are all the baptized ones in the resurrected Christ. All the others are in him too, because one cannot deny that he died for all: the Hindu, the African, the Indian, the Chinese, the white man and all the rest of the nations. If we could see with the eyes of God we would see them wending down the road of history, the way of history. Whether they know it yet or not, they are all moving into the resurrected Christ. They are all being greeted by the Lord of history whose arms are outstretched to receive them, even as the father did in the case of the Prodigal Son.

Yes, we talked about sobornost all the while in this little book of mine. Now we have met sobornost in its full reality: Father, Son and Holy Spirit who are united by the bond of a love beyond our understanding. They are so united that they are One in Three, and Three in One.

But here we also see the soil from which sobornost springs, in which its roots are deeply buried: the soil of the Most Holy Trinity. We must be united to them—to the Father!

Remember? We do have a Father, "Our Father who art in heaven," and we must be united to him, to Jesus Christ our Brother. His incarnation, death and resurrection made it possible for us to be one in the Father and with one another, made it possible to transplant some of the roots growing in the bosom of the Trinity into our hearts. We are one with the Trinity and with all men . . . all people, watering sobornost as a garden, loving God as the Holy Spirit, the Consoler, who is forever watching that this part or that is watered.

Oh, we have free will to let the plant die . . . the plant of sobornost . . . but what a tragedy! We watch the Consoler who holds the water that will revive the plant and ask for the sign of his consolation which is the water and say we do not need it. We can make it alone.

If we do so our Lady's tears will wash the plant, but she cannot restore unity among us unless we want to restore it, because we are created free. We can reject the Trinity. We can reject God the Father. We can reject our Brother. We can reject the Consoler, and we can gather the tears of our Lady and throw them away. Such is the power of men created in the image and likeness of God. "He who sees me sees my Father."

But those of us who believe in him, who have followed him, who are baptized . . . we too can reflect the face of the Father as we walk the path of the Lord Jesus Christ and rest in the arms of the Holy Spirit, for we will need consolation, holding the hands of our Lady to keep it.

This is sobornost!